Grrreat SCOTTISH DOGS

Grrreat
SCOTTISH DOGS

Alison Mary Fitt

Illustrations by Bob Dewar

BLACK & WHITE PUBLISHING

First published 2004
By Black & White Publishing Ltd
99 Giles Street, Edinburgh EH6 6BZ

ISBN 1 84502 019 7

Text copyright © Alison Mary Fitt 2004
Illustrations © Bob Dewar 2004

A CIP catalogue record for this book
is available from the British Library.

Printed and Bound in China by Best Hope Printing Company

1 Rob Roy Magregrrrrrrr

2 Bonnie Pinscher Charlie

3 Mungo Bark

4 Walter Scottie

5 The Bay City Yowlers

6 Stanley Boxer

7 Hugh MacDiarmutt

8 Alasdair Greyhound

9 Jackie Chewart

10 Jack Vet-triano

11 The Pupclaimers

12 Doggy Donnelly

13 Gordon Setter Ramsay

14 Rover Coltrane

15 Robbie German Shepherd

16 Lab C Nesbitt

17 St Bernard Gallagher

18 Alan Ruff

19 Collie Montgomerie

20 Steven Houndry

In this little book, Scotland has completely gone to the dogs!

Rob Roy Magregrrrrrr

In Magregrrrr's day, life could be 'wruff,'
But this brave Highland hero was tough,
Though he knocked off some cattle
He was feisty in battle,
Grrreat legends are made of such stuff!

Bonnie Pinscher Charlie

To the Jacobites Charlie did moan,
"It is *me* who should be on that throne!"
But defeat at Culloden
Left him sad and downtrodden,
And hopes of being King were all flown!

Mungo Bark

Up the Niger brave Mungo was bound,
In the hope that its source would be found,
But his dream died forever
On that African river
When sadly, this explorer was drowned.

Walter Scottie

To Scottie, a novelist of fame
Ideas for his 'tails' swiftly came.
To his mind they did flock,
He had no writer's block!
Now a monument stands to his name!

The Bay City Yowlers

As they yowled on the stage high above,
Screaming fans to get near them would shove,
In their cute tartan trews
Such charm they did ooze,
You could say it was just puppy love!

Stanley Boxer

Of comedians Stan was the cream,
On the box he was mimic supreme.
As the Queen he'd appear
While in panto each year
Stanley Boxer was simply a scream!

Hugh MacDiarmutt

This Scotsman whose eye-brows would bristle,
Penned many a poem and epistle.
In his ain tongue he wrote,
And most worthy of note
Is 'A drunk man looks at the thistle'!

Alasdair Greyhound

With perception this author can write,
In *Lanark* you will simply delight.
Give the telly a miss
Get your teeth into this,
And you'll find that his books have real 'bite'!

Jackie Chewart

On the race track young Jackie was King,
And much glamour to Scots he did bring.
He retired at his 'peke'
Other ventures to seek,
Now a clay pigeon shoot is his thing!

Jack Vet-triano

Though they're not in the Tate oh so plush,
For his 'people on beaches' we rush.
His paintings so bonnie
Are out-selling Monet,
What a cruftsman he is with a brush!

The Pupclaimers

Craig and Charlie, two brothers renowned,
Much acclaim for their lyrics have found.
At gigs round the world
With saltire unfurled,
The fans love their grrrreat Scottish sound!

Doggy Donnelly

On Saturday Grandstand he's there,
Presenting the day's sport with flair,
On football and more
He's got info galore
While you just sit back in your chair!

Gordon Setter Ramsay

In his restaurants savour each bite,
His cuisine is a gourmet's delight,
A perfectionist he,
His chefs can often be
In the dog-house if things don't go right!

Rover Coltrane

In Cracker Coltrane did amuse
As a shrink who was fond of his booze,
Then later big Rover
Won Potter fans over,
And as Hagrid earned magic reviews!

Robbie German Shepherd

At broadcasting Robbie's a trouper,
His Scots music programmes are super.
On a Saturday night
Take the Floor's a delight,
And paws pound from Kelso to Cupar!

Lab C Nesbitt

To the 'polis' he's just a wee pest,
His sartorial style's a string vest –
He's completely work-shy
And he'd drink Glasgow dry,
But at making us laugh he's the best!

St Bernard Gallagher

Though high on a brae lands his ball,
You won't see his face start to fall.
This great golfing hound
Up steep slopes can bound –
St Bernard's his name after all!

Alan Ruff

Alan Ruff, with his mop of brown hair,

As a goalie had 'poodles' of flair.

To get the ball past Ruff

Was just so 'doggone' tough

Scotland's rivals would yowl with despair!

Collie Montgomery

It's a thrill to watch Collie compete,
His strokes are so perfect and neat.
At his school of golf too,
There is coaching for you
If your handicap's makin' you greet!

Steven Houndry

As he skilfully cues every ball,
Snooker's golden boy crowds can enthral.
He's so cool and laid back
As he pots red or black,
His performance just bow-wows them all!